*C*all them clients, patrons, patients, guests, members – the labels don't really matter.

The fact is, they are your livelihood. They are your CUSTOMERS.

And whether or not you get and keep their business depends on how well you treat them ... how well you *walk* the customer service talk.

The How-To Handbook For
Everyone In Your Organization

Eric Harvey
and
The WALK THE TALK Team

To order additional copies of
180 Ways To Walk The Customer Service Talk
or for information on other
WALK THE TALK® products and services
contact us at
1.888.822.WALK(9255)
or visit our website at
www.walkthetalk.com

The WALK THE TALK® Company

Printed in the United States of America
10 9 8 7

ISBN 1-885228-34-1

Printed by The Graphics Group

♻ This book is printed on recycled paper.

$\mathcal{S}$pecial thanks …

… to the following members of The WALK THE TALK Team
for their contributions to this handbook:

Linda Andrus   Nancy Heindl

Juli Baldwin   Paul Hollrah

Bud Bilanich   James Johnson

Michael Bone   Anita Kasmar

Joanna Brandi   Carie Krueger

Joachim de Posada   Garfield "Gary" Lear

Renée Dye   Al Lucia

Tom Fanning   Joel Marks

Terry Fitzwater   Suzanne McBain

Dottie Gandy   Brian McDermott

Aaron Graves   Eva Peplinski

Stuart Graves   Heather Rice

Erika Harvey   Kevin Ruble

Nancy Harvey   Karl Schoemer

Nicole Harvey   Paul Sims

Barbara "BJ" Hateley   Scott Strange

Jim Welch

And a very *special* thanks to

Steve Ventura

for his creativity, encouragement,
and many invaluable contributions.

*E*ver stop to really think about what business you're in? Ask most people, and they'll say things like: manufacturing, sales, healthcare, banking, insurance, computer software, food service, hospitality, retail, etc., etc., etc. If that's the kind of answer you'd give, you'd be only half right!

Here's a one-question test: If all of your customers went away for good, would you still have a business … *would you still have a job?* Of course not! Well, that's your clue to the more important half of what you do: YOU'RE IN THE **CUSTOMER SERVICE** BUSINESS. And that means you not only need to know the right way to fix cars, write programs, run equipment, or whatever, you also need to know the right way to serve customers. You need to know it, and more importantly, you need to *practice* it.

When you look at what most organizations *say* nowadays, it's obvious that they recognize the importance of good customer service. It seems that everywhere you look you find businesses proudly touting statements and slogans like: "Customers come first," "We're here to serve," and "We go the extra mile." Sound familiar? Sure! And the irony is that while all this noble, well-intended talk is on the rise, it's apparent that the quality of service, in general, is on a steady decline.

Check your own experiences as a customer: Hasn't superior service really become the exception rather than the rule? Don't you find yourself pleasantly *surprised* when people go out of their way to serve you? Haven't you at some point, with some vendor, taken your business elsewhere because of poor service?

Bottom line: Businesses are losing customers every day because they aren't *walking* the customer service talk ... they aren't treating customers the way they say they will. That needs to change. It needs to be turned around –180 degrees. And that's what this handbook is all about. It's a guide to help you meet one of today's most pressing business challenges: satisfying and keeping the customers that pay the money that pays *your* salary. That last part – paying your salary – should be reason enough to pay attention.

As you read on, you'll find a collection (180 to be exact) of simple yet powerful techniques, strategies, practical how-to's, creative ideas, and a few things to remember – all designed to help you successfully deliver the absolute best type of service:

"WALK THE TALK" CUSTOMER SERVICE.

And now, the final question: **Why bother?** Why make any kind of special effort with customers if (and that's a BIG "if") mediocre service is enough to protect your job and paycheck? Well, the way we see it, when it comes to providing Walk The Talk Customer Service:

You owe it to the customer – the one who has <u>chosen</u> to give their hard-earned money to your business. They deserve the best you have to offer.

You owe it to your organization – the one that not only gives *you* money, but also entrusts you with its livelihood and future. It deserves the best you have to offer.

You owe it to yourself – the one who enjoys the pride, satisfaction, and reputation that comes from giving your all. YOU deserve the best you have to offer.

Read on. Serve well.

Getting Started
How to use this handbook.

180 Ways To Walk The Customer Service Talk is jam-packed with techniques, strategies, how-to's, and things to remember. In fact, there's *so* much good information, it might be a little difficult figuring out how to use it all. Here are a few suggestions to get you started:

First, read the handbook from cover to cover with a highlighter in hand. Mark any key words or phrases that you find particularly relevant and meaningful.

Next, select three ideas or action items that you wish to personally adopt. Circle the number of each item you select (1-180) and mark the pages they appear on with "sticky notes." Review these pages frequently.

Finally, each time you complete/master one of your action items, draw an "X" through its circled number and select a new item to work on in its place. That way, you'll have three ideas working at all times. Before you know it, your handbook will be filled with crossed-out numbers … and you'll be well on your way to walking your customer service talk.

ontents

**The key principles of
"Walk The Talk" Customer Service**

Master the basics

*The game of business
is very much like the game of tennis.
Those who fail to master the basics
of serving well, usually lose.*

–Unknown

1. Remember that "walk the talk" service starts with the first few seconds of the first contact. You get only one shot at a good first impression. So, greet your customers warmly. Start phone contacts with: "Thank you for calling (XYZ Company)." Start face-to-face contacts with: "Welcome to (XYZ Company)." Customers take their business where they feel welcomed and appreciated.

2. DON'T LET CUSTOMERS FEEL INVISIBLE. Acknowledge walk-up customers immediately – even if it's only to say, "Thanks for coming in. I'll be able to help you in just a moment." People will be more willing to wait patiently if you act like you know they're there.

3. When customers are lined up waiting to be served, avoid the cold and impersonal "Next!" Instead, make eye contact with the next person in line, smile, and nod your head. Most people will understand that as an invitation to step forward. If you can't make eye contact, try saying, "May I help the next person?"

4. Develop the habit of looking each customer in the eye during face-to-face service situations. Maintaining eye contact helps you focus on what the customer is saying, and it shows them that you're interested in helping them.

5. USE THEIR NAME. Get the customer's name early by asking, or by looking at their check, credit card, etc. Then use the name throughout the transaction. Use "Mr." or "Ms." unless you sense that the more personal first name is appropriate.

6. People like to have their names pronounced correctly. Make notations in your files showing the phonetic spelling of names that have unusual pronunciations. That way, you or the next employee to have contact with the customer will know the correct way to say the name.

7. TELL 'EM *YOUR* NAME. Starting service interactions with, "Welcome to XYZ Company. I'm Chris. How can I serve you?" makes the interaction more friendly and personal. The customer can connect with you as a person rather than a "server."

8. Smile every time you greet customers in person *and* every time you answer the phone. Remember, you can hear smiles as well as see them. And smiling whenever you pick up the phone will keep you positive and upbeat. Try it … it really works!

9. Never leave a customer on hold for over one minute without reconnecting with a status report. Ask if they would prefer a callback. If so, get a phone number, get a convenient time, and make sure the return call happens!

10. Don't just transfer a customer call – make sure the person you're transferring to is there <u>and</u> can answer the question or solve the problem.

11. Respect the customer's time. Never, ever make them wait for anything without offering an explanation, an apology, and an alternative to waiting.

12. Give the customer you're serving 100% of your attention. Do paperwork, organizing, and other job duties on your time rather than theirs.

13. TALK LESS, LISTEN MORE. Make it your goal to understand the customer's needs and expectations rather than "talking your way into a sale." Listen to everything the customer says as if there was a test at the end. And confirm your understanding by paraphrasing: repeating back, in your own words, what the customer says (e.g., "What I hear you saying is ...").

14. Pay attention to your body language – the unspoken, unwritten form of communication. Make a list of gestures, tone, stance, etc., that you find disturbing in others. Analyze the list – asking to what degree you may do the same disturbing things yourself. Then, make a conscious effort to avoid them.

15. Don't be a ROBOT. If you have a verbal script you need to follow, personalize the delivery ... put a little of yourself in it. Just reciting policies, procedures, and script lines makes you no different than a recording.

16. Always read back important information (customer's name, address, phone, product or service ordered, shipping and billing details, etc.) to confirm you have recorded it correctly.

17. If you make a mistake when dealing with a customer, admit it, apologize for it, fix it, and move on. Customers really don't expect you to be perfect. They do, however, expect you to be honest … and make a great recovery.

18. HONOR YOUR COMMITMENTS. Do what you say you'll do. For example: If you tell a customer you'll research why their shipment hasn't arrived and get back to them before lunch, you better follow through – even if it's just to call and say you're still working on it. Customers occasionally make plans, schedule meetings, and make decisions based on what you tell them you'll do. Fail to deliver, and they may conclude that your products and services are as bad as your word is.

19. UNDER PROMISE and OVER DELIVER! Keep your promises reasonable, but make what you provide for the customer extraordinary!

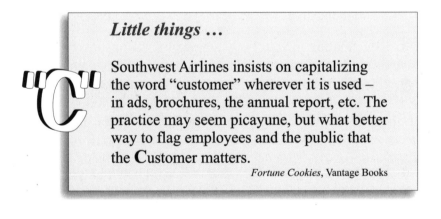

Little things …

Southwest Airlines insists on capitalizing the word "customer" wherever it is used – in ads, brochures, the annual report, etc. The practice may seem picayune, but what better way to flag employees and the public that the Customer matters.

Fortune Cookies, Vantage Books

20. Here's a biggie: Never tell a customer that you *can't* do something unless you immediately follow with a description of what you CAN do for them! Customer service is about DOING – not explaining or rationalizing what you're *not* doing.

21. DON'T KNOW? FIND OUT! If you don't know the answer to a customer's question, don't offer a guess ("I think ..."). And never end the issue with, "I don't know" or "I'm not sure." Always conclude with: "... but I'll be happy to get that information if it would be helpful for you." If they *do* request an answer, get it and get back to them promptly. Even if they say "don't bother," get the answer anyway and get back to them. They'll appreciate the extra service, and you'll have the correct answer for the next time the question is asked.

22. Set a personal goal to become an expert on the products and services you offer. Read manuals and marketing brochures; talk with product developers, vendors, and service deliverers; use the products and services yourself. The more you know, the better your service will be.

23. ELIMINATE THE NEGATIVES. Make a conscious effort to minimize the use of negative words and phrases in your service interactions. Customers do not appreciate words like: can't, won't, don't, not, no, and sorry. You need to look for every opportunity to say: can, will, do, yes, you bet, and absolutely.

24. LISTEN TO YOURSELF. Periodically tape-record your side of customer service phone calls. (Set the microphone close to your phone so you'll pick up your voice, but the customer won't be heard or recorded.) Play the tapes and analyze your performance. Hear yourself as the customer heard you. What did you do poorly that you need to correct? What did you do well that you need to continue doing? Consider asking a few co-workers to listen to the tape and give you feedback.

25. Remember that customers don't like unpleasant, last-minute surprises. Immediately inform them of any unexpected delays. Contact them if something about their order has changed (item out of stock, delivery delay, lost shipment, etc.).

26. If children are part of the service situation, pay attention to them and make them feel important. Ask their names, give them compliments, or give them something special. This will enhance the service experience for the customer and increase the likelihood that they'll come back.

27. Here are two "rules of thumb" for people in the repair business: 1) When you fix it, clean it! 2) When you're finished fixing and cleaning it, put a sticker on it that has your company name and phone number ... so the customer will remember who to call with any future problems or compliments.

28. Give every customer your very best service. Remember, you never know who you might be dealing with. Your next customer could be the president of the company, who's testing the service. They could be a reporter doing an under-cover story about your  operation. Perhaps they're your boss's spouse, who will definitely comment on the experience when they both get home. Or maybe they're a competitor looking for an excellent customer service person to steal away at three times your salary. Think about it.

29. Take abbreviated notes throughout your conversations with customers. Start by jotting down their name, and then continue by writing words and short phrases that capture the essence of what the customer is saying.

30. As you approach the end of each customer interaction, do a short recap/summary of what you discussed, what you are going to do for them, what they can expect and when, and the benefits of their purchase – so they feel even better about their decision to do business with you.

31. Always, always, ALWAYS thank the customer for their business. Tell them how much you appreciate their choosing your organization for the products and services they need. Remember, it's the customer who's paying your salary – as well as paying for: the phone you're talking on, the counter you're standing behind, the vehicle you're driving…

32. Another always: ALWAYS INVITE THEM BACK. Close your interactions with something like: "Please call again. We'd appreciate another opportunity to serve you," or a simple "Please come back and see us again." You'll be amazed at the number of customers who'll say, "I will"... and really will!

33. DON'T FORGET YOUR *INTERNAL* CUSTOMERS. Does your job involve providing services for other departments, groups, or individual employees within your organization? If so, those people are customers, too. They're *your* customers, and they deserve the same level of good service as the general public who does business with your organization.

The "Golden Rule" proposes treating customers the way *you* want to be treated. The "Platinum Rule" says treat them the way *they* want to be treated. Perhaps it's time for a new rule that's closer to the concept of "empathy." I'm not sure what precious metal to put in the name, but the rule goes like this:

Treat customers as if you were the customer!
Joel Marks

A "Crash Course" on Customer Service

The **10** most important words:
"I apologize for our mistake. Let me make it right."

The **9** most important words:
"Thank you for your business. Please come back again."

The **8** most important words:
"I'm not sure, but I will find out."

The **7** most important words:
"What else can I do for you?"

The **6** most important words:
"What is most convenient for you?"

The **5** most important words:
"How may I serve you?"

The **4** most important words:
"How did we do?"

The **3** most important words:
"Glad you're here!"

The **2** most important words:
"Thank you."

The **MOST** important word:
"Yes."

Think "relationship"

Be it furniture, clothes, healthcare ...
industries today are marketing nothing more
than commodities – no more, no less.
What will make the difference in the long run
is the care and feeding of customers.

–Michael Mescon

34. Work at developing a relationship BEFORE you address the customer's request or attempt to make the sale.

35. Use the customer's name and encourage them to use yours. That makes the service interaction more personal and relationship oriented. Most people prefer doing business with people they "know" rather than with those they perceive as total strangers.

36. USE YOUR EXPERIENCE. Think about the very best **experience** you've had as a customer. What made it so good? Now, think about your worst experience. What made it so bad? Try to replicate those positive characteristics and eliminate the negative ones in *your* dealings with customers.

37. Remember, there are two levels of relationships: Short Term – the rapport you establish during the initial service contact, and Long Term – the follow-up and periodic contact you have after the initial contact. Both are important ... both must be worked on.

38. Honor the uniqueness of each of your customers. Take the time to understand their needs, issues, and concerns.

39. Ask customers open-ended questions like, "How can I best serve you?" rather than questions that lead to simple yes or no answers. You'll not only get a better perspective on the customer's specific needs, but you'll also encourage the two-way communication that's so critical to solid relationships.

40. REPEAT WHAT'S WORKING. Think of all your clients and identify the one you have the best **relationship** with. Analyze that relationship and write down the top three behaviors you engage in that make it so good. Make it a personal goal to replicate those behaviors with as many other customers as possible.

41. Look for opportunities to compliment the customer. Saying things like, "That's a beautiful sweater," "What a great tie," "Gosh, you've got a wonderful smile" will usually produce a smile, a thanks, and the start of a relationship. If you're sincere in your praise (that's an absolute must), the customer will feel great … and you will, too.

42. Need a way to get the conversation going? When the customer gives you the name of their city, say: "That sounds familiar. Where exactly is it?" Then ask about the customer's organization: "What type of business are you in?" Pretty soon, you'll be chatting like old pals.

43. Look for, listen for, and comment on things you have in common with the customer (e.g., similar car, same home town, same name). If true, saying things like, "No kidding, I'm from that same area …" can make the transaction more alive and personal.

44. If you use, and are satisfied with, products or services from the customer's company, tell them … and thank them. If you're not satisfied with their products, find some other time to convey that message.

45. Reinforce the customer's decision to do business with you. Saying things like, "You've come to the right place!" "Good choice!" "That's one of our most popular ..." and "I think you'll really be happy with that!" will increase customer comfort and help minimize buyer's remorse.

46. Create a TREASURE CHEST. Keep a stash of recognition goodies (e.g., trinkets your organization uses in marketing, give-away products, discount coupons). Use these "treasures" whenever you want to do something special for special customers.

47. KEEP UP WITH CURRENT EVENTS. Comment on things that are happening in your customer's locale. For example: If there was a big storm close to them, ask if they were affected. If a sports team in their area won a championship, ask the customer if they're a fan – if they are, congratulate them. (If they're not, congratulate them anyway!)

48. Surprise customers with a "haven't spoken with you in a while ... hope things are going well" personal note, greeting card, or e-mail.

49. Extend a standing invitation for the customer to stop in for coffee whenever they're in your area. Just make sure you'll be able to give them 10-15 minutes of uninterrupted time if they take you up on the offer.

50. Send customers copies of magazine articles, news clips, and other information you come across that are relevant to either their business or to specific issues they're facing. Include a "just saw this and I thought you'd be interested" note. Before you throw that next junk mail brochure away, ask yourself if you have a customer who might benefit from it.

51. OFFER A TOUR! Give customers a tour of your operation. Take them around, show them how you do what you do, and let them meet some of the many other people involved in serving them.

52. Who says you can't mix business with pleasure? Most people prefer dealing with individuals and groups who appear to enjoy themselves. So, **let that cheerful sense of humor of yours come out.** Laugh. Kid a little. Make fun of yourself. Just make sure you temper it with good judgement and common sense. The best relationships are those that develop among people who are being themselves.

53. Make notes on any personal information the customer reveals (e.g., spouse and children's names, pet, birthday or big vacation coming up, sports team fan). Follow up with a call, card, or note. You'll show interest and concern, and you'll help move the relationship from customer/vendor to something closer to a friendship. And that personal touch minimizes any tendency to act like a robot that collects money and disperses goods.

54. Get a **LEG** up on relationships:

Listen for things you have in common … things to remember about the customer.

Establish rapport by focusing on the person rather than the business.

Go "outside the box" to make it special.

55. Acknowledge kindness from the customer. Say, "You're one of my favorite customers because ..." or "You're the absolute best customer I've talked with all day. Thank you for being so nice." Just like you, customers appreciate hearing good things about themselves – as long as you're honest and sincere. And why wouldn't you be sincere? These are the type of customers that make your days terrific!

56. Adopt the HAPPINESS-PLUS-ONE perspective. Whenever you get to the point where you really feel the customer is happy, look for **one more thing** to do for them. It can be something you give them, something you send them, something you say to them, or whatever. It doesn't have to be big. Even little extras can turn a happy customer into a delighted one.

57. Consider closing all new business transactions by saying, "Welcome to our family of customers!" People like the feeling of belonging. So, why not make them feel special – why not make them feel "exclusive" when they do business with you?

58. Staying with the family theme ...
GIVE THEM MEMBERSHIP CARDS.
Have "official membership in our family of
customers" cards printed in mass. (You can
really have fun with this one.) The front side
of the card has all the "This is to certify that ..."
stuff and a place to add the new customer's name. The back of the card says something like: "Whenever you need anything from our 'family,' call me. I'm standing by to serve you." And include a place for the customer server to add their name and work phone.

59. Give the customer your name and work phone. Tell them to call you personally when they need something or if they ever have a problem. You'll give them the comfort of knowing they have an "inside friend."

60. BRAINSTORM your way to better relationships. Get a bunch of employees together, in a meeting, to address the following question: *What are some creative, clever, off-the-wall, "out-of-the-box" things we could do to build special relationships with our customers and separate us from our competition?* Spend 10-15 minutes generating ideas. Then, have the group discuss the ideas and identify the best three. Finally, have the group develop a plan (who, what, where, when, how) for implementing the three ideas as quickly as possible.

61. Make sure your relationship-building activities reflect an understanding that the customer's time is valuable. They'll want it friendly, and they'll appreciate it being fun. But chances are they're not looking for a 15-minute chat about the weather. Look for the quick-hit opportunities to be personable, and then move on to serving them.

62. TAKE YOUR CUE FROM THE CUSTOMER. You *will* come across a few customers who just want to take care of business and then get out (or hang up). You know them – the ones who give short, monotone answers to your best "get the relationship going" questions. For those folks, a good relationship with you means quick, efficient, get-down-to-business service. So that's what you need to give them ... along with a cheerful smile.

CARPE MOMENTUM SERVIRE

(Semi-slaughtered Latin for "Seize The Moment To Serve")

Make it difficult
to be difficult
Dealing with customer problems and complaints.

*If you see someone without a smile,
give them one of yours.*

– Jacquelinemae Rudd

63. As long as they're not abusive, let customers with problems
vent. Don't interrupt. Telling you their complete story, and de-
scribing how upset they are, allows customers to release pent-up
negative energy. The sooner they let it out, the sooner they'll calm
down and participate more productively in the discussion.

64. BE AGREEABLE! One of the fastest and most effective
ways to diffuse customer anger is to *agree* with them. Saying,
"You've got a right to be mad," or "I can understand why you're
upset – I would be, too" can literally stop an upset customer in
their tracks. Their case has been made … the fight they expected
never happened. And, if the next thing you say is, "Let's see what
I can do to make it right," you'll immediately take the discussion
from negative complaining to constructive problem solving.

65. Ask the customer to identify the solution they would like.
Just be careful you don't say things like, "So, what do you want
me to do about it?" Use a more tactful approach, like: "We want
you completely satisfied. What would you consider to be a fair
solution?" If you can meet their request, do it! If you can't, at least
make sure you tell them what it is you CAN do.

66. DON'T PLAY THE BLAME GAME! Blaming the customer for the problem won't get you anywhere. And blaming others in your organization is bad form. The fact is that most customers couldn't care less about *your* "innocence" – they just want their problem solved. So, accept responsibility as a representative of your company and place your efforts on problem solving.

67. SNAP TO ATTENTION! Give customers who have complaints and problems your undivided attention. Stop whatever else you're doing and focus on them. And, if you're face to face, maintain eye contact and be conscious of your body language. Remember, you're trying to restore this person's confidence in your organization.

68. Two more DON'TS: Don't make excuses, and don't quote your policy manual. Once again, customers aren't interested. The absolute best thing you can do is **FOCUS ON THE FIX!**

69. USE "I" IN PLACE OF "YOU"! One way to minimize tension is to keep your *verbal* finger pointed at you rather than the customer. See if you can feel the difference between these statement combinations:

What do you need? – What can *I* do to meet your needs?
You didn't complete the form. – *I* need a little more information.
You need to call this number... – Let *me* give you a number...

70. Use the customer's name to stop abusive ranting and raving. Calmly say, "Mr. Jones," and then wait. You might have to say it again, but most people will stop when they hear their name – and they'll typically respond with "Yes?" You'll then have the chance to steer the discussion toward more productive problem solving.

71. Help the customer feel in control by asking rather than telling. Instead of saying, "I need to put you on hold while I check," try "I'd like to put you on hold so I can check … is that okay?" As long as you're doing something to help them, most customers will say, "Sure, go ahead."

72. LEAP into handling customer complaints:

> **L**ISTEN – focus on understanding their concern
> **E**MPATHIZE – imagine yourself in their shoes
> **A**CKNOWLEDGE – tell them you understand
> **P**AMPER – go the extra mile to make it right

73. Keep a notepad close by. As soon as you sense that a customer has a problem or complaint, start making notes. Customers can get testy if they have to tell (and relive) their story twice because you failed to write down the specifics the first time.

74. REMEMBER: "YOU" DOESN'T MEAN *YOU*! When customers are frustrated, they often say things like, "You screwed up my order!" Most of the time, they're using "you" to mean your organization. Occasionally, they mean you the individual – the specific representative of your organization. In neither case do they mean you, the person. How could they? They don't know you. Their frustration is *business* related … so don't take things personally. When they say "you," try hearing "us."

75. Never end with "no" or "we can't." Those represent *non-*service. Always recommend a solution or compromise.

*C*omplainers are GREAT!
They give you the opportunity
to fix their problems
and keep them as customers –
instead of saying nothing
and taking their business
elsewhere.

*B*e thankful for problems.
*If they weren't so hard, someone with less
ability might have your job!*

– Unknown

76. Be a FANTASTIC FIXER! Take pride in being able to solve customer problems. Remind yourself that anyone can handle the easy stuff – it takes a real pro to successfully tackle the tough issues. Keep a "scorecard." Every time you fix a problem for someone, put a mark on your card. The more marks you have, the more fantastic you are!

77. Develop the habit of "compartmentalizing." Insulate one customer interaction from the next. Take a lesson from professional golfers, who discipline themselves to forget the last shot and focus only on the next one. Don't let a challenging encounter spill over into the next customer contact … or the rest of your day.

78. MAKE IT A CONTEST. Think of problem solving as a game. You win by turning an upset customer around and making them happy – you lose if you lose your cool. Every time the customer says or does something negative, you counter with a positive technique. Say to yourself, "There's no way this customer is going to trap me into doing something counterproductive." The interesting thing about this game is that when you win, so does the customer. And if you lose, so does the customer!

79. Adopt the TWO-PERSON RULE. Never make a customer talk to more than two people in order to resolve a problem. If you're the second person to deal with the customer, you "own" them. Either solve the problem immediately, or get a phone number and a convenient time to call back.

80. After you've resolved a customer's complaint, put a note in their file indicating that they should receive special attention the next time they do business with you. The last thing you want is for them to have two bad experiences in a row. If they do, chances are you've lost them for good.

Interesting tidbits

On average …
Satisfied customers tell **5** people about good service they receive.
Dissatisfied customers tell **10** people about bad service received.

Hal Mather, *The Performance Advantage*

For every unsatisfied customer who complains, there are **26** other unhappy customers who say nothing. And of those 26, **24** won't come back.

U.S. Office of Consumer Affairs

The average company loses approximately **20%** of its customers each year.

Patricia Sellers, "What Customers Really Want," *Fortune*

Of customers who take their business somewhere else:
15% find *cheaper* products elsewhere
15% find *better* products elsewhere
65% leave because of poor customer service.

The Forum Corporation

"We've collected the most common service complaints, and every one of them is rooted in a lack of respect for the customer."

Leonard Berry, Director
Texas A&M University Center for Retailing Studies

Even if you achieve 95% customer satisfaction, you still have **50** customers out of every 1,000 walking away dissatisfied.

Develop an "attitude of gratitude"

It's not the employer who pays the wages. Employers only handle the money. It's the customer who pays the wages.

– Henry Ford

81. Don't lose sight of the fact that you need your company as much as it needs you, and your company needs its customers MORE than they need it!

82. PICK YOUR ATTITUDE! You know, attitude really is a matter of CHOICE. As much as we'd sometimes like to blame others (including customers) for our bad feelings, the fact is we all choose how we respond to situations. So, make picking your attitude part of your daily start-up routine. Place a sheet of paper like the one below on a bulletin board. Each morning, put a push pin next to the attitude you choose for the day. Don't put the pin next to how you *feel* – put it next to how you *choose to feel* for the day. Remember: If you choose to feel bad, you have no one to blame but you.

Cheerful/Grateful
Grumpy/Ungrateful

83. Remember why your organization exists: To serve the customer. If you ever catch yourself falling into the "if only these customers would leave me alone so I can do my job" trap, visualize what would happen if you got your wish. What would happen to you and your career if customers never "bothered" you again?

84. Never forget that customers have choices as to who they buy from. Be grateful when they choose you and your organization, and give them a reason to choose you again.

85. The PICTURE OF GRATITUDE. Keep a photograph of something meaningful in your life (family, pet, car, etc.) at your phone, cash register, reception counter, truck, or wherever you work. Glance at the picture as you begin each customer contact and remind yourself that the next person you help is really helping you pay for or support that important part of your life.

86. Be just as grateful, helpful, and considerate with small orders as you are with big ones. The same person you satisfied with a small order may be the customer who comes back and orders BIG!

87. If you don't love the act of serving, try to act the love of serving. You just might act your way to loving it.

88. Think of someone you've experienced who has a "good attitude" about customer service. Next, jot down what it is they specifically do that led to your positive conclusions about them. Finally, do your very best to model their behavior.

89. COUNT YOUR BLESSINGS! Next time you find yourself feeling stressed, overworked, or in a general "Poor me ... I can't deal with one more person" funk, think about others who are worse off than you. Picture someone in a hospital who is seriously ill; think of someone who has lost their job. Then, remind yourself that any of these people would be happy to trade places with you – and take on your problems – in a second. You'll find your situation isn't so bad, and you'll be more grateful for that next customer.

> Remember that who you're *being* is just as important as what you're *doing*. Focus on the ATTITUDE behind your behavior. You can have decent service skills and techniques, but if your attitude is out of whack, the behaviors will be close to meaningless.
>
> Barbara "BJ" Hateley

90. Is the customer always right? It's probably safe to assume that the customer is right as much as you are when you're the customer. But that really doesn't matter anyway. The fact is, the customer is always the customer. And it's your job to help them always *feel* right! The issue is not what the customer *is* as much as it is what you *do*!

91. Start your customer service staff meetings by having each person share their most recent positive experience with a customer. This "celebration" will help people learn from others, and it's a way to build and spread **contagious enthusiasm**!

92. Give yourself a pat on the back – savor your service successes. Fight the tendency to focus only on the negative. The more good stuff you celebrate, the more you'll want to do.

A letter to every employee ...

Dear Every Employee:

For now, I have chosen to be YOUR customer. And no matter what part of the organization you're in – no matter what job you perform – you are part of my customer service experience. YOU determine whether or not I'll be back.

When I come to your restaurant, office, or store – or when I call your organization – I expect to be treated well by the people who wait on me. But I judge your business by a lot more than just how I'm dealt with by the "customer service people." I look at everything. I look, and I ask questions: Is the facility clean and well maintained? Is the product or service of good quality? Did the shipment arrive on time and in good condition? Was the payment processing handled efficiently and correctly? Were the shelves well stocked and organized? Was the work scheduled appropriately? Are written communications and processes clear and easy to understand? Is the staff adequately scheduled and trained?

My list of questions goes on and on, and eventually touches the area that you're personally responsible for. You see, you are in the customer service business. And whether directly or indirectly, you do touch me.

Chances are, you'll never know me personally. In fact, depending on your job, you may never even see me. But you probably ought to appreciate the heck out of me. I am, after all, the reason your business exists. I am the reason you have a job. Do your part to make my experience a good one, and I'll be back to give you my hard-earned money again, and again. Let your part of the bargain slip because you think customer service is someone else's responsibility, and I (and my money) will go somewhere else. The choice is yours ... and mine!

Your Customer

Keep *their* best interests in mind

*Customer service doesn't come from
a manual, it comes from the heart.
When you're taking care of the customer,
   you can never do too much. And there is
NO wrong way – if it comes from the heart.*

– Debbie ("Mrs.") Fields

93. Focus on the customer's needs instead of your own. Start each day with the thought, "I want to help as many people as possible today," rather than "I want to sell a lot today" or "I hope I have an easy day." Your customers will sense your helpful attitude and they'll return.

94. FIND OUT WHAT THEY NEED! You can't meet the customer's needs until you know what they are. And sometimes the customer doesn't know what they need, either. So find out by asking open-ended questions like: "What kind of issues are you facing?" "Can you describe what happened?" "What do you need this to do?" Of course, if the customer knows what they need and want, get it for them!

95. If necessary, bend the rules a little to satisfy customers. Going beyond your authority may be challenging, but losing a customer forever is much worse ... and much harder to explain.

96. Don't push for a sale if the customer isn't ready to buy.

97. Learn to say, "Want to change that? NO PROBLEM!" Be okay with customers changing their mind about what they want – even after you've spent a ton of time processing their original order. Your time is never wasted as long as the customer gets what they want. Remember the goal: **customer satisfaction**.

98. Give customers what *they* want, not what *you* think they ought to have.

99. Help the customer save money. If dollars can be saved in the quantity ordered, in the method of shipment, or through any special promotions you have going, let the customer know. We all go back to the people who watch out for us.

100. Send handwritten notes telling key customers about special events, promotions, and sales. This personal touch will make the customer feel special and increase the likelihood that they'll participate.

101. Give customers honest estimates of "wait times" (how long they'll have to wait: for a shipment, for a dining table, to see the doctor, for a repair person to arrive, for their car to be ready, etc.). And never say, "It should be just a few more minutes," unless you're sure that's the case.

102. Become a Customer Service ACE:

> **A**ttentive to each customer and their requests
> **C**aring about their needs and problems
> **E**xcited about your services and products

103. Send your customers to YOUR COMPETITION! No, we're not nuts! Sometimes the best thing you can do is refer a customer to a competitor. If your "talk" is great customer service, and a competitor can meet a need that you can't, your "walk" needs to be a pass-along. Your customer will appreciate you looking out for their interests, and they *will* be back.

104. Follow up with customers who have special needs, or deadlines to meet, that involve your products or services. Knowing that you're on top of things will increase their confidence in your organization. And, it will make their jobs easier by having one less thing to worry about.

105. Call customers to confirm (remind them of) appointments or reservations and to give them directions. This extra touch will be greatly appreciated and can cut down on your "no shows."

106. Do whatever you can to make the final bill LESS than your estimate – even if it's just by a few dollars. The customer will be happy, and you increase the chances that they'll come back. EVERYONE WINS!

107. Don't cut customers short just because your shift is about to end. Stay with them as long as it takes. Customers *are* your business ... and their service shouldn't be affected because you want to beat rush-hour traffic ... or because your company doesn't pay overtime.

108. THROW IN AN EXTRA! Everyone loves getting more than they expected ... "getting something for nothing."

109. LET THEM TRY IT BEFORE THEY BUY IT!

110. LET THEM RETURN IT IF THEY DON'T LIKE IT!

111. Keep a list of satisfied customers who are willing to talk about your products and services. Ask prospective customers if they'd feel more comfortable talking with an actual user before buying. As a courtesy, notify the people you're referring to each time you do it ("You'll be getting a call from ..."). Don't "go to the well" too many times with any volunteer, and make sure you do something nice for these special friends who help you service new clients.

112. If you're not sure how to do something, do it the way you would if a close friend was the customer you're serving.

You'll never be able to satisfy EVERY need and request. But if customers perceive that an honest effort is being made on their behalf, you'll please most of the people most of the time.

Follow with follow-up

More business
is lost every year through neglect,
than through any other cause.

– Jim Cathcart

113. Write the following on an index card (or sheet of paper) and post it close to wherever you deal with customers:

> Customer service doesn't
> always end with the sale.
> Sometimes, it begins there.
> FOLLOW UP!

114. Make it "standard operating procedure" to contact each customer after their purchase to ensure satisfaction with the product or service they received.

115. It's imperative that you follow up with customers who had problems or complaints – even if you're confident the issue has been resolved. Contact them in 1-2 weeks just to make sure everything is still okay.

116. Tell customers you will follow-up with them. Ask them how they would like to be contacted (e.g., phone, note, e-mail, fax, etc.), and when it would be most convenient for them to receive your follow-up contact.

117. Try following THE 70/30 RULE:
Spend 70% of your time servicing new customers.
Spend 30% of your time following up with existing ones.

118. Set aside a regular, dedicated time for handling follow-up activities (e.g., phone calls, notes, e-mails, faxes). If you don't make it a scheduled event, it will probably end up as a good intention that rarely, if ever, happens!

119. Another "standard operating procedure" to adopt: ALWAYS follow up with customers to ensure shipments were correct, on time, and in good condition.

120. Send e-mails or faxes at the end of each day to notify customers that their orders have been shipped. Include a tracking number, if available.

121. Consider making your follow-up calls to key customers LESS businesslike! Instead, handle them as if you were calling a friend. Phrases like "How are you?" and "I was just thinking about you, so I thought I'd call and touch base..." can enhance your relationship and provide an opportunity to make sure that your products and services continue to be satisfactory.

122. Keep notes in each client record of follow-up calls made to that person. By doing periodic record checks, you'll be able to determine if your frequency of contact is desirable.

123. Send a personalized "thank you for your business" note whenever practical. Often, the most powerful follow-ups are those that have no agenda or purpose other than to express your gratitude.

Feast on feedback

*The only way to know
how customers see your business is to
look at it through their eyes.*

– Daniel R. Scroggin

124. Set up a customer feedback voice mail or e-mail that goes directly to the owner, president, or senior-level manager. Publicize this important feedback mechanism and encourage customers to use it. You'll get invaluable information for improving your products and services. And, customers tend to feel more comfortable doing business with organizations when they have access to "The Big Kahuna."

125. Form a Customer Advisory Board consisting of several key clients. Ask them to review and critique plans for new products and services. Solicit their ideas on how your organization can improve. Have one-year terms for Board members, with a lunch meeting each quarter at a classy restaurant in your area.

126. Put a simple (3-4 questions) customer satisfaction survey on the back of your remittance envelopes.

127. Check in with repeat clients quarterly. Develop a customer satisfaction survey that is simple and personal. Design several questions that will help you get a clear picture of what the customer would change, add, or delete in your products, services, and your customer service itself.

128. Develop a ONE-THING FEEDBACK SYSTEM. Periodically, as you conclude service situations, ask the customer: "What one thing can we do to better serve you the next time you call on us?" Record the customer's input on index cards and post them in a location where they'll be seen by the entire service staff. Bring the cards to staff meetings and discuss strategies for acting on the feedback.

129. Before asking questions like: "Was everything satisfactory?" or "Did you enjoy your ____?" make sure you know specifically what you'll say and do if the customer says, "NO!"

130. For a quick yet informative customer service survey, ask these three questions:
1. What are we doing well that we should keep on doing?
2. What are we not doing well that we should stop doing?
3. What should we start doing that we aren't doing now?

131. Remember that customer feedback is a gift – valuable information that can help improve your business. Any time a customer spends more than five minutes of their personal time doing you this favor, reciprocate with a gift, trinket, discount coupon, or some other tangible "thank you."

132. If you make specific changes as a result of feedback from a customer, send a follow-up note telling them about what you've done. Thank them for their feedback, and invite them to come back and experience the positive change they helped create.

Keep learning

*Develop a passion for learning.
If you do, you'll never cease to grow.*

– Anthony J. D'Angelo

133. Have regular meetings among customer service reps to share experiences, techniques, and "best practices."

134. SHOP THE COMPETITION. Make phone orders to competitors and have your team members monitor the calls. Inspect the merchandise and shipping container when it arrives. Pay attention to delivery times and return policies. This can be an eye opener as to what you need to change, and what you're doing better than the competition.

135. LEARN FROM YOUR FAMILY AND FRIENDS. Ask friends and family members about their experiences as customers. What are their service expectations? Where do they receive great service? What are the specific behaviors they notice in both good and poor service providers? What advice do they have for you? Takes notes on what you learn and act on the information. And don't forget to thank your sources for the free training!

136. Set a personal goal to read two books on customer service each year. Use a highlighter to identify key learning points. Then, pass your highlighted book on to others.

137. USE THE INTERNET. Participate in special interest groups and "chat rooms" that focus on customer service issues.

138. Develop a LISTEN-IN PROGRAM. Have everyone in your organization spend one hour every 2-3 months monitoring customer service situations. This will keep employees "close" to customers. And, they'll learn some good techniques from your customer service reps.

139. KEEP A "LEARNING LOG." Use a small notebook – or dedicate pages in your day planner – to record customer service ideas you want to implement. Jot down things you hear, read, or observe in others. Scan your log at the beginning of each week as a reminder of ways you can deliver superior customer service. And, periodically make copies of your log pages and share them with your co-workers.

140. Soar with your strengths! Identify your customer service strengths by asking your colleagues, friends, and customers. Then look for ways to do what you do best more often.

141. LEARN BY TEACHING. Volunteer to assist with your organization's customer service training. You'll not only develop in-depth knowledge about the subjects you prepare to teach, but you'll also be able to help others learn and grow.

142. Whenever someone on your team attends a workshop related to customer service, ask them to conduct a 20-minute presentation in which they share their key learning with the rest of the group. That way, everyone can benefit from one learning experience, and you'll maximize the bang for your training buck!

143. BE A MENTOR. Volunteer to work with new customer service employees. Share what you've learned. Remember that when the people you work with deliver exceptional service, everybody wins … including you!

Make them *want* to do business with you

There is only one boss – the Customer. And he can fire anybody in the company from the chairman on down, simply by spending his money somewhere else.

– Sam Walton

144. Provide business hours that are convenient **for the customer**. Survey your clients to determine how your current operating hours match their needs and make adjustments as necessary.

145. If you have an automated phone answering system, make sure it's "user friendly." Ask friends, colleagues, and employees to try it out. Get feedback from clients who have used it. Act on the feedback you receive. And whatever you do, ensure that your system has provisions for talking to a REAL PERSON!

146. Consider providing a service guarantee. If your customers aren't really satisfied with the service they receive, perhaps they should be eligible for a discount – or some other consideration.

147. GIVE THEM CHOICES! Provide the customer with options: payment preferences, ordering and service alternatives, shipping options, etc. Customers are usually happier when they have choices.

148. If you don't have a toll-free phone number, **get one**! If you have one, encourage your customers to use it. It will cost you more, but each call represents potential business for you.

149. If you use an answering system to receive after-hours phone calls (and you should), make sure all calls are returned first thing the next business day. Also consider creating an emergency number for customers to call if they experience problems.

150. CUT TO THE NETWORK! Invite customers in your area to a breakfast or lunch where they can discuss how they're using your products and services. Encourage discussion about successes and challenges. They'll leave feeling special and wanting to do business with you even more.

151. Create a FREQUENT BUYER CLUB. Reward repeat customers with discounts, gifts, complimentary products, or special services. Give your customers a reason to come back and they will!

152. Create an "Our Friends Directory" in which you list businesses and business people that are good clients of yours. Encourage your employees to do business with the people who do business with you. Let your customers know you've done this, and you'll ensure that what goes around continues to come around!

153. Make sure that the product or service the customer is buying is top quality. Superior service is about more than just how customers are treated. It's also about giving them real value in exchange for their money.

Take advantage of technology

Think about it. Right now, a whole generation of young [customers] in the United States has been brought up to take computers for granted. Pointing with a mouse is no more mysterious to them than hitting the "on" button on the television is to their parents.

–Andrew S. Grove

154. Instead of playing music on your phone "on hold" function, consider playing recorded messages about your products and services, and other information that can benefit the customer.

155. Automate your order-taking system. This will allow you to: 1) expedite the process for your customers; 2) quickly quote prices, taxes, and shipping charges; 3) monitor your inventory so you can tell customers if items are in stock; and 4) minimize human errors.

156. Consider installing contact management software. There are many good and inexpensive programs available for creating a customer database. This will allow you to automatically track customer purchases, log customer information, and even remind you when it's time to follow-up with specific clients.

157. Create a computerized troubleshooting database that customer service reps can refer to when addressing customer problems. Include categorized diagrams, flowcharts, and process instructions that can quickly be located.

158. GET THE OTHER ADDRESS. Always ask customers if they have an **e-mail** address. If so, make sure you add this information to your files. It will allow you to extend special offers, discounts, or value-added information in the future via this efficient, convenient, and cost-effective medium.

159. Send special customers electronic greeting cards ("e-cards") that are free through many sources on the Internet.

160. Develop electronic newsletters that are e-mailed to customers on a regular basis. This is a great way to keep your clients updated on your industry, your organization, your products and services, and other clients who have useful information to share.

If you don't have a website, GET ONE! If you do have one ...

161. Refer customers to your website if they seem hurried or unsure of what they want. Tell them they can find out more about your offerings at their convenience.

162. Establish a "bulletin board" on your website so customers can communicate with one another. This form of cyber-networking – linking up customers electronically – provides another value-added resource for the people you serve.

163. Consider putting "hyperlinks" on your website that allow customers to link to/connect with businesses that offer products and services that complement your own. Establish reciprocal arrangements with those businesses so they'll do the same for you.

164. POST FAQ'S. Add a Frequently Asked Questions section to your website or electronic newsletter. Have your service reps identify common questions and issues that come up in their dealings with customers – along with the correct answers or responses. By posting this, customers can become more informed and alleviate common concerns on their own … 24 hours a day.

165. Make it possible for customers to buy products or order services directly over your website. You'll attract people who prefer to deal with computers, and you'll provide around-the-clock service to your customers – regardless of your staffed hours.

166. COLLECT CYBER FEEDBACK. Use your website to collect feedback on your products and services. Customers will have another vehicle for communicating with you, and you'll get invaluable information that you can use for product and service improvements.

167. Post phone-center employee pictures and bios on your website. This will give customers the option of seeing and finding out about who they're dealing with on the other end of the phone. This adds a personal touch to a typically impersonal medium.

168. Develop an in-house CYBER SUGGESTION BOX. Ask employees to submit ideas for innovative ways to use technology to provide better customer service. Recognize all submissions and reward people for ideas that are implemented.

169. Don't let technology replace person-to-person kindness. Websites, e-mails, and the like are efficient tools. But face-to-face helpfulness is still the most valuable customer relations strategy of all.

The difference is PEOPLE

A guest checking out of the Polynesian Village resort at Walt Disney World was asked how she enjoyed her visit. She told the front desk clerk that she had a wonderful vacation, but was heartbroken about losing several rolls of exposed film. She was particularly upset over the loss of the pictures she had taken at Disney's Polynesian Luau, as this was a memory she especially treasured.

Now understand, The Walt Disney Company has no service standards covering lost luau snapshots. But the hostess at the front desk understood and embraced Disney's philosophy of caring for their guests. So, she asked the woman to leave her a couple of rolls of fresh film, promising that she would take care of the rest.

Two weeks later the guest received a package at her home. In it were photographs of the entire cast of the luau show, personally autographed by each performer. There were also shots of the Magic Kingdom parade and fireworks – all taken by the hostess on her own time, after work.

Writing Disney, the guest stated: "Never in my life have I received such compassionate service from any business establishment."

The lesson here is clear: Magic service moments don't come from rule books or policy manuals. They come from PEOPLE who care – and from a culture that encourages and models that service attitude from top to bottom.

The Speaker's Idea File

Focus on the people who focus on the customers

Motivate them, train them, care about them, and make winners out of them... we know that if we treat our employees correctly, they'll treat the customers right. And if customers are treated right, they'll come back.

– J. Marriott Jr.

170. The first step in providing good customer service is **hiring the right people**. Make your selection process part of your customer service strategy. During interviews, ask questions like: "If you get this job, describe the kinds of things you will do to provide superior customer service." Also, pose hypothetical customer service situations and ask candidates to describe how they would handle them.

171. Make Customer Service a part of ALL written or verbal job descriptions – no matter the function or level. In hiring interviews, orientation, and on-the-job training, emphasize that *everyone* is in the customer service business. And make sure that each employee understands how they directly or indirectly "touch" the customer.

172. Clarify your expectations about customer service. Condense them to 3-5 key principles, give them a label (e.g., "The Big Four" or "The Game Plan"), and communicate them to everyone. Then, have follow-up meetings with individual employees to ensure that they know exactly what is expected of them.

173. Provide training and resources (like this handbook) to help your people develop customer service skills. Make sure the training reinforces your specific service expectations.

174. Remember that people do what's *ex*pected when it's *in*spected! Include Customer Service in all performance evaluations. Prior to conducting evaluations, ask employees to submit a list of the specific things they've done to help provide superior customer service.

175. Adopt the attitude that your employees are your customers, too. Give them the same respect and attention that you want them to give to *their* customers. Satisfied employees tend to produce satisfied customers.

176. Walk awhile in *their* shoes! Keep in touch with your customers and your employees by spending at least two hours each month working alongside customer service employees.

177. Go on a PARALYZING POLICY HUNT! Ask employees to identify policies and procedures that get in the way of providing good service. Then do your best to update, modify, or eliminate as many as you can.

178. Make sure your customer-contact employees know how much discretion they have (i.e., ability to discount or comp goods, services, shipping, etc.) when addressing customer complaints and problems. Encourage them to do whatever is necessary – within reasonable limits – to make the customer happy … without having to come to you for permission first.

179. Give each employee a number of certificates worth X dollars (say, $5) that they can give to anyone in the organization who really goes the extra mile to contribute to superior customer service. At the end of each month or each quarter, employees can turn in the reward certificates for cash or merchandise. Let employees reward each other ... it's too important a job to be left up to management alone!

180. CELEBRATE SUCCESSES! Recognize and reward employees who provide exceptional customer service. Share their stories with others. This will motivate the entire team. Motivated employees go above and beyond for your customers ... and for the organization.

We celebrate the development of this handbook! Our hope is that it and we will serve you well.

A closing thought...

*W*alking the customer service talk is not about perfection. Rather, it's about being better than yesterday and being better than the competition.

The Authors

Eric Harvey, President of The WALK THE TALK® Company, is an internationally known author, consultant, and speaker in the areas of values-based business practices and organizational change. His 28 years of professional experience are reflected in his nine highly acclaimed publications, including the best-selling *Walk The Talk ... And Get The Results You Want.*

The WALK THE TALK Team is a collection of highly respected authors and speakers, facilitators, employees, business associates, and colleagues – all with extensive experience in the field of customer service as consultants, educators, practitioners ... and as customers themselves.

The WALK THE TALK® Company

Since 1977, The WALK THE TALK Company has worked in partnership with clients worldwide to help them develop and maintain organizational practices that are in sync with their company's values and strategic objectives. As your primary source for Values Based Business Solutions, we offer a full range of resources and services – all designed to help you and your organization turn shared values like Respect, Responsibility, Integrity, and Commitment into value-added results.

To learn more about our high-impact training resources, keynote presentations, and consulting services:

call us at

1.888.822.WALK(9255)

or visit our website at

www.walkthetalk.com

Four easy ways to order
180 Ways To Walk
The Customer Service Talk

PHONE
Call **1.888.822.WALK(9255)** toll free
or 972.243.8863
Customer Service Hours: 8:30 a.m. to 5 p.m. CST
Monday through Friday

WEBSITE
www.walkthetalk.com
Visit us online 24 hours a day

*OR, complete the order form on the back
and return it by either of the following:*

MAIL
The WALK THE TALK Company
2925 LBJ Freeway, Suite 201
Dallas, Texas 75234

FAX
972.243.0815

Would you like your organization's name and logo to
appear on books you purchase?
Ask us about private labeling for large volume orders.

Call us today! 1.888.822.9255

180 Ways To Walk The Customer Service Talk
Order Form

1-99 – $7.95 each
100-999 – $7.45 each
1000-4999 – $6.95 each
5000-9999 – $6.45 each
10,000 or more – $5.95 each

Copies _____

Book Total $ _____

* Shipping and Handling + $ _____
(Continental U.S. – $4.00 plus 7% of "Book Total" above)

Subtotal $ _____

Texas Only – Sales Tax (8.25% of Subtotal + $ _____

TOTAL $ _____

05XX

*SHIPPING & HANDLING:

Outside the continental U.S., please call 972.243.8863.

Orders shipped ground delivery to be received in 7-10 business days.
Next business day and second business day delivery is available.
Call 1.888.822.9255 for information.

☐ I'm interested in bringing the "Walking The Customer Service Talk" message to my organization. Please contact me.

Name (MR/MRS/MS) _____

Title _____

Organization _____

Street Address _____
(Do not use P.O. Box)

City_____ State_____ Zip_____ Country_____

Phone (required to process order) (   )_____ Ext. _____

Fax (   )_____ e-mail _____

Purchase Order Number (if applicable)_____

☐ MasterCard   ☐ VISA   ☐ (card)   ☐ Check or Money Order Enclosed
(Payable to: The WALK THE TALK Co.)

☐ Please Invoice
(orders over $100 only)

Account Number_____ Expiration Date _____
(month/year)

Signature _____